Breads

Arepa bread

Babka

Bagel

Baguette

Banana Bread

Brioche

Challah

Chapati

Ciabatta

Cornbread

Focaccia

Injera

Multigrain

Naan

Paratha

Pita bread

Potato bread

Pumpernickel bread

Rye Bread

Soda Bread

Sourdough

White Bread

Wholemeal

www.ingramcontent.com/pod-product-compliance
Lightning Source LLC
Chambersburg PA
CBHW041526070526
44585CB00002B/98